New Paths of The Law

by

Roscoe Pound

**FIRST LECTURES IN THE ROSCOE POUND
LECTURESHIP SERIES**

THE LAWBOOK EXCHANGE, LTD.
Clark, New Jersey

ISBN 9781584776727 (hardcover)
ISBN 9781616192648 (paperback)

Lawbook Exchange edition 2006, 2012

The quality of this reprint is equivalent to the quality of the original work.

THE LAWBOOK EXCHANGE, LTD.
33 Terminal Avenue
Clark, New Jersey 07066-1321

*Please see our website for a selection of our other publications
and fine facsimile reprints of classic works of legal history:*
www.lawbookexchange.com

Library of Congress Cataloging-in-Publication Data

Pound, Roscoe, 1870-1964.
  New paths of the law : first lectures in the Roscoe Pound
lectureship series / Roscoe Pound.
      p. cm.
  Originally published: [Lincoln] : University of Nebraska Press, 1950.
  ISBN 1-58477-672-2 (alk. paper)
  1. Law. I. Title.
K561.P68 2005
340--dc22

                                                      2005006060

Printed in the United States of America on acid-free paper

New Paths of The Law

by

Roscoe Pound

**FIRST LECTURES IN THE ROSCOE POUND
LECTURESHIP SERIES**

THE UNIVERSITY OF NEBRASKA PRESS

1950

Printed in the United States by the

Printing Division of the University of Nebraska

Contents

FOREWORD

Foreword

The lectures comprising *New Paths of the Law* were delivered at the University of Nebraska on April 24-26, 1950. They mark the opening of the lectureship established in honor of Roscoe Pound by the members of the Nebraska State Bar Association and the alumni and friends of the University.

Dean Pound is a native Nebraskan, a graduate of the University of Nebraska and a former dean of its College of Law. He is universally recognized as one of America's ablest and most distinguished jurists. His accurate and extensive learning in law and the social sciences, his clear grasp of the practical problems of lawyers, courts, and administrative agencies, his rare talent for written and oral exposition, his enthusiasm for improving the administration of justice, his passion for truth and plain speaking—these qualities have combined to earn for him a permanent place among the world's legal scholars.

The lectures and writings of Dean Pound have covered a wide range of subject-matter and still serve today as guideposts, pointing the way in the development of the law. The present lectures are a notable addition to these works. They are a timely reminder that although all roads may lead to Rome, all paths the law may take do not have a common destination.

NEW PATHS OF THE LAW

I

THE PATH OF LIBERTY

 L AW must be stable and yet it cannot stand
still." With these words I began a series of lectures in another institution almost a generation ago. It then seemed
to me that stability was required not only by the exigencies
of the economic order, which rested long-term undertakings
upon confidence in the possibility of reasonable prediction,
but as well by the rooted aversion of the free man to having
his will subjected to the arbitrary will of another. Change
was inevitable because the life which is to be ordered is a
continuous adjustment to an environment of which change
is a constant feature. It seemed therefore that we were con-
fronted with a problem of finding and maintaining a balance in which stability and change had equal place, neither
left out and neither overweighted. Today, in an era which
has divided the indivisible and is continually successful in

1

doing what had been thought to be the impossible, it is not unnatural that there should be those who would eliminate one side of the balance and dispense with stability. The ends which are attained through stability are held negligible in the ideal society and the ends which are promoted by unfettered will, changing with each case, are held paramount. But this comes to conceiving of progress from a society in which law is the chief agency of social control to one in which the will of the magistrate or administrative authority has replaced law. In the ideal society, says Paschukanis, there will be no law, or rather but one legal precept, namely, that there are no laws but only administrative ordinances and orders. Speculation about how an ideal relation among men will be reached in such a society, however, is something for the political philosopher rather than for the lawyer. I think and shall be speaking of the regime of adjusting relations and ordering conduct by the systematic employment of the force of a politically organized society. This regime, which continental jurists call the legal order, is one meaning of the term "law." The paths taken by law in this sense to attain its end or purpose is to be my subject.

On other occasions I have urged that the end or purpose—at least the immediate end or purpose—of this regime is to secure as much as may be of the whole scheme of interests, that is the whole scheme of men's desires or demands involved in living together in civilized society, with the least friction and waste. On the analogy of industrial engineering, I have called this a process of social engineering. It calls upon the jurist to find and develop the jural postulates, the presuppositions as to reasonable expectations incident to life in civilized society, which obtain in the time and place. Conflict and competition and overlapping of men's desires and demands and claims, in the formulation and assertion of what they take to be their reasonable expectations, require a systematic adjustment of relations, a reasoned ordering of conduct, if a politically organized society is to endure.

From the time of Epicurus philosophers have argued whether there are limits or on the other hand there are possibilities without limit. Whether the universe or, as we must say today, the universe of universes is without limits or is limited was one of the insoluble antinomies of pure reason propounded by Kant. Experience seems to have shown limits of effective action of the legal order in the pursuit of its end. Yet legal history shows a continual widening of the circle of recognized interests and continually more effective means of securing the interests recognized. To take out of many possible examples two, which are conspicuous in the sixty years since I was admitted to the bar, the so-called right of privacy and the vested right of the industrial laborer in his job illustrate how wide extensions in the area of recognized interests may be achieved without impairment of stability. It may be that much of what appears to be significant change may be in result largely new names for old ideas and procedures. For example, the motion to dismiss and motion for judgment, which in our new rules of federal procedure have replaced the demurrer, suggest Mark Twain's statement of the Homeric problem: Homer was not written by Homer but by another man of the same name. Recent pre-trial practice is very like the oral pleading of the fourteenth century, out of which grew the elaborate system of written pleadings we knew from Blackstone, which we had simplified more and more till we are having to go back to the Middle Ages to find out what is really to be tried—in order to bring the trial to the real points as to which the parties are at issue.

Very much more significant are changes in the direction, the course, and character of what following Holmes in the days of historical jurisprudence, we may call the paths of the law. In different times the end or purpose of the legal order may be looked at in different ways. Different paths toward the end may be pursued. The path pursued in any time or place may be clearly laid out and may lead in a definite direction toward the end as it is then conceived. At another time it may be less clearly laid out. It may hesitate between different aspects of the end and for a time may not lead assuredly to the assumed end. The path followed, the way it is laid out, the direction of its approach to the end, and the way the end is conceived of may make changes under the surface of the law, in the sense of the body of authoritative grounds of decision which are also norms or models of conduct, and thus gradually work profound changes in law both in the sense of the legal order and in the sense of the body of authoritative legal precepts in accordance with which the legal order is carried on.

From the last decade of the last century a change in the path of law had begun to be manifest. Today it is increasingly manifest. But whereas we knew with certain assurance whither the path that began to be pursued in the sixteenth century and was well laid out in the nineteenth century was leading, there is no such general agreement upon the end or purpose toward which we are now moving or by what path the end is to be reached. In the medieval beginnings of our legal order we held that the keeping of the peace was the end of the formative legal order. In the later Middle Ages and in the formative modern era the end was thought to be, as the Greeks and following them the Romans had held it, orderly maintenance of the social *status quo;* earlier thought of as calling for certainty and uniformity in the adjustment of relations and ordering of conduct to be attained through rule and form, and later thought of as assuring a prevailing of good faith and moral behavior attained through reason. Culminating in the nineteenth century the end was taken to be promoting and maintaining a maximum of opportunity for free individual self-assertion brought about by equality of secured liberties and security from culpable interference by others.

In the maturity of law in the nineteenth century equality meant equality of opportunity for free individual self-assertion. Security meant security from interference with that free self-assertion beyond what was required to maintain the like security of others. But the meaning of these two much-used words has been changing. Marx taught the latter part of the last century to mean by equality equality in satisfaction of material wants and today men think of equality in satisfaction of all the desires involved in life in civilized society. More recently security has been coming to mean security from all the ills that flesh is heir to—not merely aggression or culpable conduct of others, not merely interference with free opportunity, but want, and fear, and frustration, and one's own improvidence. But of this later.

There is little in a name. It is a name but not necessarily a description. But we may with reasonable truth call the path which modern law began to follow in the sixteenth century, the path in which its footsteps were firmly planted in the nineteenth century, the path of liberty. Indeed the era of discovery, colonization, development of new areas, and exploitation of natural resources from the sixteenth to the nineteenth century was *par excellence* an era of opportunity. There were lands to discover, aborigines to subdue, wildernesses to make into farms and later to people with cities, treasures of the earth to discover and exploit, new seas to sail, new avenues of adventure, of commerce, of achieving distinction seemingly without limit, until at least the end of the century and in America until the end of the first World War. America was the land of opportunity for peoples all over the world and a new type of frontier developed in the older settled part of the land as immigrants came in to take up the labor which the descendants of the pioneers had given up and thus raised new opportunities for the newcomer eager to advance his economic position. Opportunity calls for liberty. It calls for unhampered free individual self-assertion to develop its possibilities. Thus it is no accident that America, pre-eminently the land of opportunity, chose and pursued and developed in law the path of liberty and has on the whole kept to it while it was being less trodden or even given up elsewhere.

Magna Carta was put in the beginning in the first law book published in this country. It was relied upon in the pioneer case on freedom of the press in which in 1734 a Philadelphia lawyer successfully withstood arbitrary action of a royal governor. It was the basis of argument in American opposition to the Stamp Act. As its principles had been developed in Lord Coke's commentary and expounded by Blackstone, it was the main reliance of the colonists in the controversies that led up to the Revolution. The Declaration of Rights of the Continental Congress in 1774 declared as its purpose to assert and vindicate the rights and liberties of the colonists and claimed for them that they were entitled to the common law of England. Despite hostility to all things English during and in the years immediately after the Revolution, the several states as they adopted constitutions after the Declaration of Independence made the common law the rule of decision in their courts. Also they framed and adopted bills of rights which in their significant provisions are bills of liberties. In the formative era of our law legal thinking was characterized by an ultra-individualism, an uncompromising insistence upon individual interests and individual property as the focal point of jurisprudence.

Few doctrines of the common law in the last century were more irritating in the transition from a rural agricultural to an urban industrial society, than those of assumption of risk and contributory negligence as applied to employees in industry. They were, however, by no means repugnant—indeed they were congenial—to thinking in terms of opportunity and liberty. The employee was a free man. He chose for himself. So choosing, he elected to work in a dangerous employment in which he ran a risk of being injured. Very well. He was a free man. Let him bear the loss. As it was put in Carter's lectures as late as the first decade of the present century, one must stand or fall by the consequences of his own conduct.

In the eighteenth century American lawyers began to identify the common-law rights of Englishmen with the natural rights of man. The result was to give an extreme individualist direction to the path of liberty which the common law had been following in the era of opportunity in Tudor and Stuart England and was following in the land of opportunity in America. In both its ethical aspect and its political aspect the eighteenth-century theory of natural rights was thoroughly individualist. As a theory of inherent moral qualities of persons it was based on deduction from the nature of an abstract isolated individual. As a theory of rights based upon a social compact, it thought of natural rights as the rights of individuals who had entered into a contract apart from which there would be no law and nothing for the law to maintain. In either view law exists to maintain and protect individual interests. This was so perfectly adapted to be a philosophical theory of the doctrine of the common-law rights of Englishmen that we need not wonder that the founders of our political and judicial systems and legal thinking, who were studying Coke and Blackstone on the one hand and the French and Dutch publicists on the other, believed they were reading about the same things. In 1774 the Continental Congress claimed the common-law rights of Englishmen. In 1776 in the Declaration of Independence the Continental Congress claimed the natural rights of man. Yet each claimed essentially the same things. It followed that the common law which we claimed as our heritage and developed in the formative era of our legal and political institutions was taken to be a system of giving effect to individual natural rights. It was taken to exist in order to secure individual interests not merely against aggression by other individuals but even more against aggression by state or society. It followed also that the bills of rights, declaratory of natural rights, were likewise declaratory of the common law. Thus our nineteenth-century law was set firmly in the path of liberty.

Extension of the category of liberties, of conditions of legal hands-off or legal non-restraint of natural faculties of action, was regarded as the direction of progress of the legal order. It was said that any restraint was required to be justified and the only permissible justification was to show that the restriction promoted more liberty than it restrained. This idea is very prominent in judicial discussions on liberty of contract fifty years ago. We were told that natural persons did not derive their power to contract from the law. Hence whatever the state may do in limiting the power of a corporation to make certain contracts, because the corporation gets its powers from the state, it may not limit the contractual capacity of natural persons, who get their power from nature, so that nature alone may remove it. Another court, in passing adversely upon legislation against company stores, said that any classification limiting contracts for payment of wages was arbitrary and unconstitutional unless it proceeded on the "natural capacity of persons to contract." Another, in passing on a similar statute, denied that contractual capacity might be restricted except for physical or mental disabilities. Another held that the legislature could not take notice of the *de facto* economic subjection of one class of persons to another in making contracts of employment in certain industries, but must be governed by a theoretical jural equality.

Our constitutional legal polity was set up by strong believers in the path of liberty. The constitution was felt to be in a direct line of historical continuity from Magna Carta, through the Petition of Right, the English Bill of Rights of 1688, the Declaration of Rights issued by the Continental Congress in 1774, and the Declaration of Independence. Its characteristic feature was the common-law doctrine of the supremacy of the law; the doctrine that, in the phrase imputed to Bracton in the beginning of the common-law system, the King is under no man but under God and the law; that all acts of public official or private individual alike are subject to judicial scrutiny to ascertain whether they are within the limits recognized by law, and that lawmaking itself, as restraint upon free individual action, must keep within the limits of common right and reason as the law of the land. In the Middle Ages the common-law courts had made clear to the King that he could not, like the King of France, interfere by private letter with the course of justice in the courts. They had held that the freedom of the church, guaranteed by Magna Carta, could not be impaired by Parliament in attempting to alter the canon law in its province or to make lay functionaries into spiritual persons by statute. Fortescue in the fifteenth century had compared the security of individual liberty in England with the subjection of the individual to the king in France. A long and hard struggle with the Stuart kings had produced a gospel of the doctrine in Coke's Second Institute which, supplemented by Blackstone's exposition of its teachings, was accepted by Americans in the struggle with the government at Westminster that culminated in the Revolution. The long line of decisions in the common-law courts from 1578 to 1701 in which enforcement of acts of Parliament against common right and reason was denied, the requirement in the colonial charters that colonial legislation conform to the common law, and the acceptance of Coke's Commentary as an authoritative exposition, culminating in a line of decisions of the highest courts of the states between 1780 and 1787, in the pronouncement of the Federal constitution in 1788 that it was the supreme law of the land, and in the establishing of judicial power over unconstitutional legislation in 1803, seemed, in the reign of faith in historical continuity in the nineteenth century, to have put security of liberty of individual self-assertion as the alpha and the omega of our polity.

Not the least significant feature of the common law as it developed in America in the nineteenth century was its attitude toward the ruling power of politically organized society. Toward king, legislature, and plurality of the electorate the common law has continuously and consistently opposed its doctrine that the powers are to be exercised in accordance with the law of the land. When the fundamental law set limits to their authority or bade them exercise their authority in a defined way the common-law courts have refused to give effect to their acts beyond those limits. When the king in the fourteenth century sent out a man to collect the fifteenths granted him as what we should now call taxes, and the collector distrained cattle, the property of a subject, for nonpayment but did not show a warrant, the subject was allowed to replevy the cattle. The king's taxes could only be collected in the manner prescribed by law. Historically this goes back to the medieval idea of the relation of lord and man and so of king and subject and of the reciprocal rights involved in that relation. Along with the doctrine of judicial precedent and trial by jury, this doctrine of the supremacy of the law became one of the three distinctive characteristics of the Anglo-American legal system. It became definitely established as a result of the contest between the courts and the crown in the sixteenth and seventeenth centuries. It was reinforced in America in the contests between the colonies and the home government which culminated in the Revolution. Out of these contests grew the idea of law as standing between politically organized society and the individual and guarding the individual against arbitrary infringement of his liberties by those who exercise the authority of government. The idea became one of protection of the individual against government instead of protection of the individual by government, the conception of the relation of the individual and the state with which we are now familiar.

"All power corrupts," says Lord Acton; "absolute power corrupts absolutely." The absolute power of the king in the old regime in France, the misgovernment of the Stuarts in England, the abuse of absolute power in government of the American colonies from Westminster were ever before men's eyes in the formative era of our institutions. Security against oppression by the agencies of government is a constant theme in our law books down at least to the end of the last century. To that time at least the beginner in study of law read about it in Blackstone and the elementary books of a generation ago were full of it. Ratification of our federal constitution came near failing because of fear that a central government, too far from the people in their local governments, would be an instrument of oppression. Only the assurance of addition of a bill of rights to the Federal constitution enabled its ratification, and a bill of rights put in the constitution of every state attests persistent distrust of government and fear of misuse of its powers.

In law we rely upon experience and reason. As I have been in the habit of saying, law is experience developed by reason and reason tested by experience. For experience we turn to history. For reason we turn to philosophy. Philosophically a doctrine that the sovereign, whatever its form and in all its agencies, was bound to act upon principles, not according to arbitrary will, and was bound to conform to reason instead of being free to follow caprice, was based upon an idea of a universal ideal natural law, binding all men in all places and at all times, demonstrated by reason and inherent in the nature of man as a rational creature. As this natural law was discovered in the nature of the individual man, it was highly individualist. It assumed a necessary opposition of society and the individual and reinforced the doctrine of law as standing between the two in order to give necessary protection to the latter.

Professor Corwin in a recent book has called attention to the decadence of this legal-political doctrine. It reached its height in the first decade of the present century and, after a generation of struggle between courts and legislatures, fell with the failure of the courts to stop workmen's compensation legislation.

Juristic thinking both in Europe and in America long held the development of legal precepts and doctrines in the path of liberty. Indeed in America legislation began to stray from that path and finally to abandon it long before the science of law in this country was ready to give up the claim that it was the one and only true path. Let us notice how it seemed to our science of law in the last century.

One of the three problems with which the science of law concerned itself in the nineteenth century was the interpretation of legal history. The nineteenth century was the century of history in the development of political and legal thought. It turned to the philosophy of history for a key to its problems and to the history of philosophy for its philosophy. Thus the interpretation of legal history became a crucial matter for the jurist. Of the six interpretations which were urged two had chief influence, namely, the ethical interpretation used by the metaphysical jurists of continental Europe and the political interpretation urged by jurists of the historical school in England and in the United States. Each was an idealistic interpretation. Each sought to find the idea which was unfolding or realizing itself in the history of law not only in the body of received precepts but as well in the body of institutions by and in which justice is administered.

In the ethical interpretation the idea which is realizing itself, which is unfolding in legal history, is the idea of right. Kant had provided a metaphysical formula of right which was at hand to be made into a formula of law. As I have said elsewhere, Savigny put Kant's definition of right in terms of ordering the activities of free beings, coexisting in a condition of free contact with each other, by means of rules determining the boundaries within which each might securely exercise his freedom. This gave us a theory of law. It was a theory adapted to a time which valued opportunity and so liberty. Throughout the century social and legal philosophy was troubled to reconcile government and liberty. Men were troubled by the antithesis of a system of adjusting relations and ordering conduct by systematic application of the force of a politically organized society on the one hand, and of a regime of individual freedom resting on the autonomy of the human will. Kant's formula of right was an attempt at an absolute and universal solution. Beginning with the individual consciousness as the ultimate datum, and conceiving of the task of the legal order as one of reconciling conflicting free wills of conscious individuals independently exerting their wills in the different activities of life, he formulated a theory of justice in those terms as a reconciliation through universal rules whereby the will of each actor may coexist with the will of all others in action. This became, in one form or another, the idea of justice for all of the nineteenth-century schools. With the passing of the era of opportunity it has passed also.

Philosophically the ethical interpretation represented the influence of Kant upon historical jurisprudence, the growing and finally dominant type of science of law in the last century, resulting in an interpretation of legal history and hence of law in terms of Kant's theory of right. The political interpretation represents the influence of Hegel. It is an interpretation in terms of Hegel's proposition that right is "freedom as an idea." Hegel was formulating a conception of the end of law—of the purpose for which the legal order is established and maintained. Directed toward its end it realizes the idea of freedom, the idea that "existence generalized is existence of the free will." Looked at legally and politically the idea is freedom or liberty.

Maine's famous generalization of legal history as a progress from status to contract is the most important phase of the political interpretation in its practical consequences in the hands of courts and lawyers. His generalization is the political interpretation put concretely in terms of legal institutions. It came to be universally accepted in Anglo-American juristic thought and governed even beyond the end of the century in American constitutional law.

We must remember that "truck acts," or legislation against company stores, were held unreasonable and unconstitutional by a long line of state decisions between 1880 and 1911. A Workmen's Compensation Act was held unconstitutional by the highest court of New York in 1911 and a minority of the Supreme Court of the United States considered such legislation arbitrary and unreasonable and consequently unconstitutional in 1920. To a generation brought up in the tenets of the historical school and trained in the doctrine of progress from status to contract it was not thinkable that the contractual powers of free men should be restricted by enacting that men of full age and sound mind in particular callings should not be able to make agreements which other men might make freely. As that generation saw it such statutes vainly sought to turn back the wheels of progress. They were arbitrary attempts to restore status. This was not confined to the courts. In the first decade of the present century James C. Carter's *Law: Its Origin, Growth, and Function,* a series of lectures by a leader of the bar which had much vogue for a time, preached the doctrine of the historical school and Maine's theory of the progress from status to contract.

Moreover the rival schools of jurists held in their own fashion to the Kantian theory of justice. Bentham held that happiness, the end of political and legal institutions, consisted in being free. To him no less than to the historical jurists the maximum of free individual self-assertion was the highest good. Spencer had, as he tells us, never read Kant. But starting from the Comtian teaching that reality in the social sciences is in social laws comparable to the physical laws with which the physicist has to do, he came independently to Kant's formula of justice as a "law of equal freedom." Three centuries of free opportunity had intrenched that idea in the thought of the time.

But long before the century was out new modes of thought were suggesting that new paths for the development of law might yet be discovered or laid out. Some of what was projected was new application of what had come to be the staple of political and juristic theory. The economic realist, the philosophical anarchist, and the social individualist were at outs radically with orthodox juristic theory. Yet they argued from the same postulated conception of justice and idea of the end of law as metaphysical jurist, historical jurist, utilitarian or Comtian positivist. The highest good was the maximum of individual free self-assertion. But it was not to be attained as thinkers in the main current of philosophical thought since Kant had believed. The idea of liberty was not to realize itself in the Kantian legal order. The economic realist would use liberty realized in doing away with the economic order and starting afresh. The philosophical anarchist would do away with all ordering of conduct by the force of politically organized society. The social individualist would use a maximum of government to bring about the maximum of liberty which the metaphysical jurist, the historical jurist, the utilitarian and positivist had believed called for a minimum of government. There was still general adherence to the direction of the path of liberty if not to the path toward liberty as laid out. Yet the era of opportunity was felt to be over. Satisfaction of wants, with opportunity to satisfy them, began to be urged and new types of what we call social philosophies arose to give direction to the development of law.

Beginning in 1878 there was Jhering's Social Utilitarianism. Then in 1895 Stammler's Neo-Kantianism and in 1901 Kohler's Neo-Hegelianism. In France Gény's neo-scholasticism and Duguit's sociological natural law followed. Philosophy of law was moving toward a different path not yet fully marked out. In America Comtian sociology as developed by Ward was, even at the beginning of the present century, moving cautiously but definitely away from Spencer's grafting of Kant upon Comte. But before all this American law, in advance of American legal science, was moving also. Legislation was steadily multiplying restraints upon individual free self-assertion. Beginning about 1880, it had taken on great proportions by 1900. Judicial decision began to go in the same direction particularly in restraining what the French call abusive exercise of rights. By the end

of the second decade of the present century the transition
to what jurists call the socialization of law had become so
marked that a new stage of legal development had become
recognized in continental Europe, in England and in
America.

Of the twelve types of radical departure from the nineteenth-century idea of maintaining the liberty of each so far
as it does not infringe the liberty of all, now well established
and undoubted, only a few types and few examples under
each can be looked at here. I choose some of the first to be
urged and first to be established and a few later extensions
and applications. Some have been brought about by judicial
decision. Others have been provided by legislation. The
number of types and the examples under each are still growing. The main categories or types have doubled in number
in a generation.

First we may note restrictions on the owner's liberty of
using his property. Sixty years ago, when I was a student in
law school, this was beginning to be agitated with respect
to spite fences, spite wells, and spite diversion of surface
water. At that time Professor Gray, who had an exception-
ally sound judgment as to what American courts of that
day would hold, did not hesitate to pronounce the few decisions limiting the owner's *jus utendi* to a beneficial use
unsound and at variance with the principles of the common
law. Free exercise of the owner's will, no matter what his
motive, was to be upheld so long as it did not impair the like
free exercise of the will of any other owner with respect to
his property. The owner was the best judge of what was to
him a beneficial use. Today free exercise of the *jus utendi*

out of spite is forbidden either by legislation or by judicial decision as universally as it was upheld four generations ago. Next came zoning laws, replacing restrictions voluntarily imposed by owners through covenants and restrictive agreements. For a long time the courts refused to recognize these laws, considering them arbitrary and unreasonable interferences with liberty and property with no basis in promoting public health, safety, or morals. They are now universal and universally upheld. The same story may be told of legislation against billboards and advertising devices impairing the scenery along highways. Today the owner may not even maintain ornamental rows of cedar trees along the driveways leading to his house if they harbor a rust which may infect a neighbor's apple trees.

According to Coke, the oracle of Anglo-American common law, liberty of enjoying (*jus fruendi*) is nothing less than ownership. Here, if we impose restrictions, we restrict both liberty and property. Sixty years ago it had begun to be questioned whether the courts could or should interfere with an owner's pumping out all the percolating water beneath his land and selling or using the water off of the land. Today an idea of securing a social interest in the conservation of social resources has led to restriction of the owner's *jus fruendi* to use of the water upon his land. Here even a legitimate benefit to him in sale or use of the water is no more valued than his claim to free exercise of his will. The same idea of securing a social interest in the conservation of social resources has been used to justify legislation restricting the taking of oil and gas from beneath the surface of one's land. It is felt that free exercise of the owner's *jus fruendi* must not be permitted to go to the extent of wasting important media of satisfying the wants of others in times to come. Hence use of the natural gas beneath the surface of an owner's land to make lamp black, in which process eighty-five percent is wasted, where the whole could be used for heating a neighboring municipality, has been held something which legislation may limit or forbid. In England a good while ago rent control made a fundamental change in the polity of security of liberty and property, and a regime of rent control came to us also in the exigencies of a housing shortage during the World War and shows signs of becoming permanent.

Power of disposition, the power of transferring one's property to another or to create property interests in it in favor of others by suitably manifested intention, was regarded by philosophers no less than by lawyers in the last century as a necessary incident of ownership. Indeed Kant regarded it as so essential to ownership that he used it in philosophical explanation of ownership based on original occupation and appropriation. But limitations of this power by legislation began in America a good while ago in the homestead laws forbidding alienation of the family home without the consent of the wife. Later legislation in some states forbade a husband who had bought the household furniture with his savings before marriage subjecting it to a chattel mortgage without his wife's consent. Some states forbid the husband's assigning of his wages without his wife's consent. Recently we have seen statutes fixing or restricting the prices at which property may be sold. Power to restrict the use of land conveyed in order to benefit land retained had become well recognized especially through the establishment by courts of equity of equitable servitudes. They could be created by manifested intention in the form of covenants or restrictive agreements or plans shown to purchasers at the time they acquired their interests. Today this exercise of the owner's *jus disponendi* is limited by judicial decision to the extent that restrictions as to race or color of purchasers will not be enforced.

Liberty and property are joined in the bills of rights as equally to be secured against arbitrary deprivation. We have noted the tendency to multiply limitations on liberty in connection with property. Another type which has been growing enormously is restriction upon liberty of contract. Bentham thought that the public was in nothing more vitally interested than in allowing men freely to contract and in holding them to their contracts when and as freely entered into. Maine taught that whereas in the beginnings of law men's rights and duties were annexed to their status or position before the law, the progress of the law was toward leaving them to fix their rights and duties for themselves by free agreement with their fellows. But, if Maine's generalization is sound, the law has been progressing backward for two generations, slowly and cautiously for a time but with increasing momentum in the present. It will be enough to remind you of the restrictions which have practically deprived public utilities of liberty of contract with their patrons, and of legislation imposing standard policies upon insurers and limiting the warranties which can be provided for, and the judicial decisions as to warranties, which sometimes go further. Legislation as to contracts with employees began to limit the liberty of contract of both employer and employee in the eighties of the last century. It has gone far today. Also in England there has been a striking change of judicial attitude toward covenants not to compete with the employer or not to enter the service of a competitor. The whole doctrine as to contracts not to exercise the calling for which one has trained himself has taken a new turn in the present century.

Finally we may look at the development of restrictions on the power of a creditor or an injured party to exact satisfaction. It will be enough to remind you of exemption of homesteads from execution, of exemption of personalty of the head of a household, of legislation providing for judgments payable in installments, of the doing away with deficiency judgments, and of the extensions of the benefit of bankruptcy.

It should be noted that much of the foregoing admits or has appeared to admit of explanation on the basis of the general security, security against interference with opportunity. But such explanation was often specious and is less and less possible as we pass to the third decade of the present century. New attitudes toward liberty, new ideas as to the claim to free individual self-assertion, have become increasingly manifest. New paths are at least beginning to appear. I suggest calling one the humanitarian path. It is the path indicated by a new idea of security. I suggest calling the other the authoritarian path. It is a path of increased subjection of individual self-assertion to state control, becoming substitution of regimented co-operation for individual initiative and moving toward the omnicompetent bureau state.

II

THE HUMANITARIAN PATH

WHAT I am calling the humanitarian path, the path directed to a newer and broader idea of security, seems to be indicated for a time when the world has ceased to afford boundless conspicuous opportunities which men only need freedom to take advantage of, in order to be assured of satisfaction of their reasonable expectations. Where there are opportunities in every land for freely exerting one's will in pursuit of what he takes to be the goods of existence, security means an ordered competition of wills in which acquisitive competitive self-assertion is made to operate with a minimum of friction and waste. Where this ordered struggle for existence does not leave opportunities at hand for everyone, where the conquest of physical nature has enormously increased the area of human wants and desires without corresponding increase in the means of satisfying them, equality ceases to mean equality of opportunity. Security ceases to mean security of freely taking advantage of opportunity. Men assert claims to an equality of satisfaction of wants which liberty in itself cannot afford them. They begin to assert claims to security in living a full life in the society of the time and according to its standards, which liberty in itself cannot give them. A desire for an ideal relation among men which we call justice leads to thinking in terms of an achieved ideal relation rather than of means of achieving it. Instead of picturing men as ideally free to achieve it we begin to picture them as ideally in that relation. Security then is security from all that keeps men from that ideal relation and keeps many of them far from finding themselves in it.

The ideal of a world in which all can find themselves in this relation we call the humanitarian ideal. A path of legal development directed toward that ideal we may call the humanitarian path.

After all we have to recognize that as the world is made all organic beings are subject to the Darwinian struggle for existence and that civilization is a mitigation of an inevitable competition. Hence the law has to provide a system of liability whereby disturbance of the ordered social existence is repaired and the ideal relation among men maintained by imposing and enforcing duties of reparation. This is not all of the task of law. But it is a large and crucial part. The divergence of a humanitarian path from the old path of liberty is strikingly brought out by the rise of new theories of liability.

When the mission of law was maintaining and promoting liberty, the problem of jurist and lawmaker seemed to be to keep in balance free exercise of the will of each with like free exercise of will by all others so that individual activity ought not to be restrained except to allow like activity of others. The line of adjustment was taken to be prevention of and reparation for culpable interference with person or property. Equality and security were expected to be assured in that way. We may call this the fault theory of liability. From this, while the law was still in the path of liberty, there was a gradual shifting to an idea of maintaining the general security as the basis of liability. But the security thought of was security against menace to safety, health, peace and order, to acquisitions under the prevailing social and economic order, and to the stability of the legal transactions on which the economic order depends. With the coming of a new conception of security new theories of liability were required. The two which seem to belong to law proceeding in a new humanitarian path I am calling the insurance theory and the involuntary Good Samaritan theory. In practice, however, the former is used to justify what in reality is the latter.

It is worth while to trace the development of these theories. When I studied the law of torts in 1889 the theory of liability was a very simple one. Tort liability was a consequence of fault. One who culpably caused damage must repair it. In the days of analytical-historical jurisprudence, when legal development was proceeding in the path of liberty, such was the accepted doctrine. It is true that on the Continent the *culpa* principle as it was called was coming under attack. In the common-law world some survivals in Anglo-American law of an old absolute liability for caused damage gave trouble, and as far back as 1865 an English decision had built a new category of tort liability upon them. Controversy over this case began when Chief Justice Doe in New Hampshire in 1873 rejected it in a vigorous opinion, accepted in New York, New Jersey, and Pennsylvania in the ten years from 1876 to 1886. This and doubts cast upon the English case at home as well as the consensus of text writers seemed in 1890 to have settled the matter. At that time one could have said there were only two things to consider: culpability and causation. But in the twenty years from 1896 to 1916 four states, beside two which had at first accepted it, had followed the English rule. Also the English courts, in spite of the views of eminent English text writers, had not merely adhered to it but were showing a disposition to extend it which has since become well marked. The controversy became acute in the fore part of the present century. Thus the doctrinal lines came to be well laid out and the new category, though in dispute, seemed to have maintained itself. Accordingly, accepting it, I undertook in 1921–1922 to work out a theory of liability based on three postulates and a corollary of one of them, with which I was content for two decades. I became troubled about the subject again in about 1942, but in the fifth edition of my *Outlines* in 1943 was not able to satisfy myself that I could formulate a further postulate and justify it from the law as it appeared to stand. I am by no means sure that I can do so now. But I am convinced that a recasting of the theory of liability is about to be required and that one may at least indicate what we shall have to consider in recasting it.

Let us look first at the development of theory of liability down to 1900. In doing this we must remember that philosophical theory of this subject begins in the rationalist nattural law of the seventeenth and eighteenth centuries, is developed in the metaphysical-historical thinking of the nineteenth century, and is looked at with much suspicion by a strong group of jurists of today. It would be idle to pretend that what we now see as the presuppositions of the law of wrongs in the past was present in the minds of lawmakers and judges and jurists at the time in the form in which we may now put it. But from the time of the classical Roman jurists, from Augustus to the third century, jurists have been much concerned with philosophy of law. They believed in what they were doing and strove to do it according to the pattern of principles. We do them no wrong when we see in what they did a continuous development of principles representing experience developed by reason and reason tested by experience.

If we may attribute theory to the beginnings of law in the two great systems which divide the modern world, it may be said that the first theory of liability was in terms of a duty to buy off the vengeance of him to whom an injury had been done either by oneself or by something or someone in one's power which or whom one would protect against vengeance. It was put strikingly in an Anglo-Saxon legal proverb or maxim: "Buy spear from side or bear it." In other words buy off the feud or fight it out. One who has caused an injury or stands between an injured person and his vengeance by protecting a kinsman, a member of his household or a domestic animal which has wrought an injury, must compensate for the injury or bear the vengeance of the person injured. As the development of the legal order puts down the feud, payment of the composition becomes something the injured person can exact. It becomes a duty of the person responsible, not his privilege. In a case of injury by persons or things in one's power or under one's protection, it becomes a duty of composition alternative to one of surrendering the offending person or animal. In time the composition came to be measured in terms of the injury rather than in terms of the vengeance to be bought off. Composition for vengeance becomes reparation for injury. Recovery of money by way of a penalty for a delict is the historical starting point of liability in Roman law and the idea of a penalty of reparation came into the modern Roman law. The plea of not guilty in the action of trespass at common law tells a like story.

Later a moral idea of liability based on fault replaced the primitive idea of liability as a substitute for composition. The theory of a law of nature, discoverable by reason, of which the positive law was but declaratory, involved a doctrine that law was declaratory of morals, that the legal and the moral must be identical. Moral responsibility was legal liability. The significant thing in delict seemed to be the moral duty to repair an injury caused by wilful aggression. But with the development of society the general security was no less affected by negligence, by subjection of others to unreasonable risk of injury through want of due care. In Roman law this was taken care of by the doctrine of Aquilian *culpa,* liability on the analogy of the *Lex Aquilia,* an old statute of the Republic providing for damage done wrongfully, a juristic equitable development to cover cases of fault not extending to intentional aggression. Fault could include both intentional aggression and negligence. In the era of natural law, in the modern Roman law, the theory of legal liability became a moral one: one who has been at fault must repair the injury due to his fault. It culminated in a famous text of the Code Napoléon: "Any act whatever done by a man which causes damage to another obliges him by whose fault the damage was caused to repair it."

In the common law, absolute liability in an action of trespass *vi et armis* for directly caused injury to person or property hung on into the seventeenth century and only disappeared as the analytical distinction between intentional aggression and negligence superseded the procedural distinction between trespass and trespass on the case. But at the end of the sixteenth century the theory of natural law was making headway in England also. In Lord Cromwell's case, in 1578, which Coke tells us was the first case in which he appeared in court as counsel, he persuaded the Court of King's Bench to hold that a statute was against common right and reason and so void where it provided that "those who do not offend are to be punished." On like grounds many state courts at the beginning of the present century held Workmen's Compensation Acts unconstitutional. The basis of tort liability must be fault. Such was the established teaching as well in common-law jurisdictions as in those which derived from Roman law. It is, as one might put it, the juristic *status quo* from which we must start in consideration of theories of liability in the law of today.

Natural law, as it was understood in the seventeenth and eighteenth centuries, was given a death blow by Kant at the end of the eighteenth century. Blackstone had done it lip service. But it got no real foothold in Anglo-American juristic thinking and the metaphysical philosophical jurisprudence which succeeded it on the Continent, while it influenced English and American text writers indirectly through the Pandectists and the historical jurists, never took root in the English-speaking legal world. Nevertheless philosophy of law was not to be kept down. It has had a rebirth in the present century. In the last decade of the nineteenth century and first decade of the present century a number of forms of social philosophy began to give useful ideas for a period of growth of the law. I am no Hegelian or Neo-Hegelian. But I have found Kohler's idea of the jural postulates of the civilization of the time and place very useful. In 1922 I undertook to formulate five jural postulates, that is five presuppositions of life in civilized society which people take for granted in their every day life so that the law seems to give effect to them as presuppositions of the legal order. Three of them were recognized in the nineteenth century as behind the law of liability to repair damage to others. They may be put thus:

1. In civilized society men must be able to assume that others will commit no intentional aggressions upon them. To this we must add a corollary. One who does anything which on its face is injurious to another must answer for injurious consequences unless he can justify by identifying what he does with some recognized social or public interest. This corollary was cautiously suggested in the latter part of

the nineteenth century, argued vigorously and no less vigorously denied in the first decade of the present century, and is by no means universally accepted. But I am satisfied it represents truly the law of today. Those who contested it overweighted the individual claim to free self-assertion.

2. In civilized society men must be able to assume that others will act reasonably and prudently so as not, by want of due care under the circumstances, to cast upon them an unreasonable risk of injury.

3. In civilized society men must be able to assume that others who maintain things or employ agencies, harmless in the sphere of their use but harmful in their normal action elsewhere, and having a natural tendency to cross the boundary of their proper use, will restrain them or keep them within their proper bounds. This postulate was a battle ground of the law of torts in the fore part of the present century. I submit that the Restatement of the Law of Torts by the American Law Institute justifies my including it in a list of accepted jural postulates.

Accordingly we may say that at the end of the first half of the present century one was liable for (1) intentional aggression upon the personality or substance of another unless he can establish justification or privilege; (2) negligent interference with person or property—*i.e.,* failure to come up to the legal standard of care whereby injury is caused to the person or property of another; and (3) unintended nonnegligent interference with person or property of another through failing to restrain or prevent the escape of some thing or agency which one maintains or employs that has a tendency to get out of bounds and to harm.

That this last category is not to be referred to negligence as established by *res ipsa loquitur* is shown by the liability for acts of servants or agents referable to a power but not to authority, the giving of the power resulting in setting up a person harmless in the sphere of his use as servant or agent but potentially harmful in normal action out of that sphere, and having a natural tendency to go beyond the bounds of his use. Here the liability is not to be explained by the *alter ego* theory of agency. The master is not represented by the servant who in the scope of his employment goes beyond the limits of his authority. Moreover such things as Blackstone's explanation of liability for cattle breaking loose without fault or wrongfully turned loose by a stranger, by saying that escape shows conclusively that they were not kept with due care, perverts the whole theory of negligence. The liability is not made to flow from negligence but the negligence flows from the legal imposition of liability. Indeed it has been argued that liability under the second postulate is not necessarily liability for fault. The standard of care is objective. One may not be able to live up to it. His act may be negligent in that he has not acted up to the standard prescribed by law and yet the natural limitations of his intelligence or his congenitally slow reaction time cannot be attributed to him as faults. The most that can be said is that if he chooses to act without being able to come up to the standard, that choice may be regarded as a fault.

On the other hand, as the common law had been, there could be no recovery of damages if the injury was caused in whole or in part by the injured person's own fault or if it was due to no one's fault. As to the first of these propositions, the Roman law and civil law following it divided the loss. Also long ago the courts began to cut down the rule as to contributory negligence and legislation has gone still farther. As things are now one is not at any rate wholly barred by his own contributing fault. The other proposition had come down from Roman law. Where injuries resulted without anyone's fault it was taken for granted that each of us must bear the risks which are inevitable in human existence. The first inroad upon this proposition was made in workmen's compensation when the employer was made liable for injuries in accidents in the course of employment occurring without fault of anyone. Here there was an extension of the third postulate. But a movement has been going on beyond that postulate and beyond its analogy and on a wholly different presupposition which may result in remaking the whole theory of liability.

The three foregoing postulates and consequent theoretical bases of liability belong to the type of government which maintains peace and public order and upholds the general security and free opportunity. In the English-speaking world, until the present generation, security has meant security from aggression or fault or wrong-doing of others. Today the term security is being used to mean much more—how much more it is not easy to say. But certainly it is made to include security against one's own fault, improvidence, or ill luck or even defects of character. At any rate government today attempts much more than it did in the era to which my three jural postulates belong. There comes to be an extension of the third postulate beyond its basis in the general security. Indeed there is more than extension. There is emergence of a new idea and building a new proposition upon it. All new ideas, until experience has brought about a firm grasp of them, are likely to give us caricatures for a time in their experimental development. Thus a developing humanitarian idea seems to think of repairing at someone's expense all loss to every one, no matter how caused. It seems to presuppose that in civilized society everyone may expect a full economic and social life. To fulfill this expectation, to guarantee the expected full economic and social life, the law seems more and more to be called on for every victim of loss, and for anyone who for any reason cannot keep the pace of attaining the full measure of his expectation, to play what I have called an involuntary Good Samaritan, to pull him out of the ditch, bind up his wounds, set him on his way and pay his hotel bill.

Forty years ago this began to be urged in the form of what was then called the insurance theory of liability, a humanitarian addition to the teachings of the past, according to which injuries or losses which are the lot of human existence should be insured against by some form of general sharing of the burden. It was assumed that this could be done by imposing liability immediately upon someone more able to bear the burden who could then pass it on to all of us or to the public by recouping it in charges for services or adding it to the cost of production in charges for things produced or manufactured.

In one phase of this humanitarian movement there has been a real and immediate shifting of the burden from the luckless individual who has been injured to the public at large. It used to be that the state could not be held for injuries to individuals through the wrongful acts of public officers. The officers who wrought the injury were personally liable to repair it. But throughout the world there has for a generation been a tendency by legislation to provide that public funds shall respond for injuries to individuals in the course of operation of governmental agencies. Legislation in America has been extending the doctrine of *respondeat superior* to the government. Here, just as in the case of injuries due to wilful or negligent action of servants of public utilities or of great industrial enterprises done in the course of their employment, the wrong-doing servant is seldom able to satisfy a judgment for damages in this time of multiplying limitations upon the power of creditors or injured parties to exact satisfaction of judgments for debts or damages. The proposition is that losses incidental to services performed for the benefit of all of us should be borne by all of us. If we adopt Duguit's teaching that the state is simply a great public service company, the extension to it of liability under the doctrine of *respondeat superior* is understandable.

Here, however, as in the case of liability of private employers for what is done by their employees in the course of their employment, there is liability only for a wrong done. There has been no extension to the state of absolute liability on the ground of causation without fault. Social security, health insurance, unemployment insurance, and old age pensions may be moving in at least a parallel direction. But they do not come under any category of legal liability. Also legislation has increasingly in the interest of the general security created offenses which dispense with criminal intent and imposed penalties for creating danger to health or safety although the offender has used all due care and has knowingly done nothing more than put on the market a carefully manufactured article, fully inspected and in itself in no wise dangerous, which nevertheless bursts or otherwise develops a defect and causes injury.

It is now proposed to extend civil liability without fault not only to these cases but to many more.

One of the earliest cases of extension by judicial action was the doctrine of the family automobile, the doctrine, as one court put it, that "where a father provides his family with an automobile for their pleasure, comfort and entertainment, the dictates of natural justice should require that the owner should be responsible for its negligent operation, because only by doing so, as a general rule, can substantial justice be attained." It was said that the principles of agency had nothing to do with such cases. They went wholly upon principles of natural justice. Some critics said at the time that ownership of an automobile indicated such affluence that a distribution of the economic surplus was called for. But the main purpose was probably maintenance of the general security. Nine states adopted the doctrine while fourteen (four of them after receiving it at first) rejected it. Later legislation imposing liability of the owner of an automobile for negligence of others using the car with his consent arrested judicial development of this sort of liability.

Recent proposals for judicial extension of absolute liability are: Abrogation of the requirement of negligence in case injury is caused to an ultimate purchaser of a manufactured article by something which may be referable to the condition of the article when it left the manufacturer's hands; abrogation of the category of independent contractors and applying *respondeat superior* to injuries through their negligence as well as those due to negligence of an agent or servant; and abrogation of the requirement of causation, so that, for example, if a man committed suicide by throwing himself under a properly operated but rapidly moving truck, the owner of the truck would be liable to the dependents of the deceased. Some of these propositions are put forward to maintain the general security. Some are advanced upon the insurance theory. More and more such things are urged on a purely humanitarian basis.

On the whole the fullest exposition has been given by a proponent of change of the law as to liability of a manufacturer so as to do away with the requirement of negligence. In a recent case involving application of the now familiar rule of *MacPherson v. Buick Motor Company* one of the outstanding state judges of today, in a concurring opinion, proposed extension of the liability of manufacturers for injuries to purchasers of manufactured articles made to be sold in the market, put in circulation accordingly, and ultimately acquired by the person injured. The proposition cannot be put better than in the exact words of the opinion: "I believe that the manufacturer's negligence should no longer be singled out as the basis of a plaintiff's right to recover. In my opinion it should now be recognized that a manufacturer incurs an absolute liability when an article that he has placed on the market knowing that it is to be used without inspection, proves to have a defect that causes injury to human beings."

This goes beyond the third of my jural postulates, the jural postulate as to things on the land constructed and maintained with all due care, of the rules as to trespassing cattle, of the rules as to wild animals escaping without fault or negligence of their keeper and the like. Under that postulate the defendant must at his peril restrain any object or activity that has a tendency to get out of hand and do damage. Even if he takes all due care he is liable for something he maintains getting out of hand and doing damage. But here he is not maintaining anything and nothing has got out of hand. He has put something on the market intended to go through a number of hands and ultimately reach a purchaser who will use it. If in this activity he fails in any respect to exercise due care and subjects others to unreasonable risk of injury, he is liable for injuries resulting from his negligence. If the defect causing the injury existed latent when he put the article on the market, if he up to that time had complete control of it, and if the defect could not have existed and been undetected except in ordinary experience through negligence, then the ordinary principle of negligence supplemented by *res ipsa loquitur* will suffice for a satisfactory result. But if all we know is that when the article got into the hands of the plaintiff it proved defective and plaintiff was hurt, with nothing to show how or when the defect developed nor to demonstrate that it must have existed in the defendant's hands, we have to find a new principle of liability.

It must be conceded, however, that the manufacturer may anticipate some hazards and guard against the recurrence of them as the purchasing public cannot or cannot easily. Accordingly the opinion quoted from argues thus: "Those who suffer injury from defective products are unprepared to meet its consequences. The cost of an injury and the loss of time or health may be an overwhelming misfortune to the person injured, and a needless one, for the risk of injury can be insured by the manufacturer and distributed among the public as a cost of doing business." As to the power of the manufacturer to insure, one might remark that those who buy automobiles can have and probably very generally carry accident insurance. This is not equally true of those who drink Coca-Cola or other carbonated drinks, which seem to account for most of the cases for applying *MacPherson v. Buick Motor Co.* in the recent reports. But all the establishments that put carbonated soft drinks on the market are by no means great corporations with ample means of procuring insurance, and the argument as to ability to pass the loss on to or distribute it among the public is by no means so convincing as it could be a generation ago.

It is true the opinion quoted limits the proposition. It says: "The manufacturer's liability should, of course, be defined in terms of the safety of the product in proper and normal use, and should not extend to injuries that cannot be traced to the product as it reached the market." Why? If the injury can be traced to the product as it reached the market and until that time was under the exclusive control of the manufacturer, *res ipsa loquitur* will take care of the plaintiff, so far as according to the proposition, as limited, he ought to be taken care of. But perhaps the argument is framed also, as the concurring opinion indicates, upon a theory of warranty running with the product. This, however, has no basis in analysis or in history. And if it is to be put on the ground of social expediency, it is a serious question whether so fundamental a change in the basic theories of the law should not be left to the legislature. If his reasoning reported in the paragraph just above this one is sound, it should make no more difference whether the case can be brought on a theory of warranty of quality running with the chattel or on one of absolute liability so that negligence of the manufacturer need not be shown. One can't help asking whether in such case the underlying idea is not that the manufacturer can stand the loss better than the person injured, which may depend upon many things in individual cases. If I am not to be my brother's keeper but am to be his insurer, so radical a change in the social order should be left to legislation rather than be achieved by judicial decision.

It should be noted that workmen's compensation does not go so far as the proposition we are considering, since it only covers injuries and losses in the course of the employment, although both administrative agencies and courts are tending to make that category very elastic. Also workmen's compensation has been coming to extend widely to cases of injury through fault of the employee himself which were at first excluded. Moreover projects are now being urged to turn over the whole subject of traffic accidents on the highways to an administrative board to be dealt with on the analogy of workmen's compensation, and indeed to extend beyond that analogy.

In support of the proposition we are referred to the absolute penal liabilities imposed by the Pure Food and Drug Acts and like legislation. This legislation is directed to maintaining the general security by putting heavy pressure upon the manufacturer to use the highest diligence in supervising the process of manufacture and choosing and inspecting the materials used and inspecting the finished product. As the penal liability is absolute the only escape can be a maximum of care and diligence which will so far as possible preclude defects. But if the general security is what is aimed at, is it not sufficiently upheld by the penal legislation? Why in addition impose an absolute civil liability for perhaps hundreds of thousands of dollars damage without fault? This liability added to that for negligence and that attached to negligence may put an unbearable burden upon enterprise. Once more one cannot help feeling that the analogy and the argument from the Pure Food and Drug Acts are make-weights and that the rise of the service state and the humanitarian theory of liability are in the end the real basis of such projects.

The French Civil Code and modern codes and legislation in the civil law would reach a result very like that of our *respondeat superior* on a theory of fault in employing, retaining, or failing adequately to supervise employees. But the circumstances of employment today make the fault idea inapplicable. Hence there is a general tendency to refer the legal doctrine only to an idea of maintaining the general security by extreme pressure upon the employer. Accordingly the opinion under consideration refers its proposition to the third of the three suggested postulates of liability and, as has been said above, vouches American Pure Food and Drug Acts and might vouch much British legislation also. Still, as has been pointed out above, that does not meet the proposed extension of the doctrine of *MacPherson v. Buick Motor Co.* by eliminating the element of negligence. An idea that all of us should bear the losses and injuries which potentially afflict each of us seems to be called for. But under the circumstances of life in the welfare state, in which the cost of government has become enormously multiplied and all manner of heavy demands upon already over-burdened public revenues appear to preclude adding any more, there is inevitable reluctance to press the idea to its conclusion by direct and immediate imposing upon government the repairing of losses and injuries without fault of anyone.

As has been suggested in another connection, this is met today, and the opinion I am discussing so meets it, by a proposition that an employer is able to pass the loss on to the public in the form of charges for services or in the prices charged for manufactured articles. Shall we, then, formulate another postulate of liability: "Men must be able to assume that losses and injuries without fault of anyone, which are part of the ordinary experience of life in society, will be borne ultimately by society through imposing liability for damages upon those able immediately to bear them and to recoup them from the public through charges for services of public utilities or through including them in prices charged for manufactured products."

But in the bureau organization of the service state of today the proposition as to passing damages for losses incurred by no one's fault on to the public by way of employer or public utility or industrial enterprise is fallacious. One bureau or commission fixes rates for service. Another fixes or may be fixing prices. Another has control of wages and hours. A

jury or some administrative agency fixes responsibility and
assesses the damages or the amount of accident compensation. Each of these agencies operates independently, subject
to no effective coordinating power. Those that control rates
and prices are zealous to keep the cost to the public as low
as may be. Those that control the imposition of liability on
employers are apt to be zealous to afford the maximum of
relief to the injured or to their dependents. With continual
pressure upon industry and enterprise to relieve the tax-pay-
ing public of the heavy burdens that our recent humanitarian
programs involve, the practical result is likely to be that the
burden is shifted arbitrarily to the most convenient victim.
There is very little if any validity in the proposition that compensation for loss and injury without fault of the utility or
enterprise is passed on to the public.

What seems to be developing as a jural postulate is: "In
civilized society men are entitled to assume that they will be
secured by the state against all loss or injury, even though the
result of their own fault or improvidence, and to that end
that liability to repair all loss or injury will be cast by law
upon some one deemed better able to bear it."

What is this but the Marxian aphorism: "To everyone
according to his wants; from everyone according to his
means"? It is also argued that the tendency of jurors to
render verdicts on the basis of what is substantially the foregoing suggested postulate is a reason for frank out-and-out
recognition (by expressly imposing absolute liability) of
what has long been the law in action in these cases. There
is merit in looking the facts of life squarely in the face. But
are we looking squarely at all the facts if we turn to a whole-

sale establishing of liability without fault in the belief that by doing so we are ourselves taking on the burden of repairing all loss and damage suffered by our fellow men? If leaving the luckless victim of loss and injury attributable to wrongful causation by no one to bear the loss is unsatisfying, yet achieving of high humanitarian purposes by the easy method of using the involuntary Good Samaritan as the Greek playwright used the god from the machine is not edifying. There ought to be a better method of making the legal order effective for our humanitarian ideals than that of Robin Hood or that of the pickpocket who went to the charity sermon and was so moved by the preacher's eloquence that he picked the pockets of everyone in reach and put the contents in the plate.

It has never been easy for the law to expand to the exigencies of newly perceived and recognized ideals. Much experimentation, much trial and error, are inevitable in the process. The law has long been moving toward more stress upon the social interest in the individual life and the law of torts is thus subjected to strain in the endeavor to attain and maintain a balance between the general security and the individual life which has long been disturbing the criminal law. It may be that we must recast our analytical scheme of obligations. We can retain, on what we used to speak of as the contractual side, contractual obligations strictly so called, official obligations arising from an office or calling, restitutional obligations imposed to prevent unjust enrichment of, or unmerited acquisition of, benefits by one at expense of another, and fiduciary obligations involved in relations of trust and confidence. On the other side, on what we used to call the delictual side, we are given pause. Shall we add another category to delictual obligations strictly so called? Or shall we make a threefold classification? Shall we say contractual, delictual, and humanitarian? It is only procedural thinking that has been leading us to treat obligations (shall I say?) *ex humanitate* with obligations *ex delicto*. Or shall we say that to set up this additional category will require us to exceed the limits of effective legal action? Not all of social control can be achieved through the law. I can conceive of administrative agencies as means whereby society may attain ideal humanitarian results much better than by the courts.

Please understand me, I am not here to preach against the service state. The society of today demands services beyond those which the state, which only maintained order and repaired injuries, could perform. Administrative agencies promoting certain aspects of the general welfare are with us to stay. It may be that some of these newer services may be performed according to law by the state. It may be that others may be performed by methods outside the law administered not by the courts but through administrative agencies. It may be that some are unattainable through the state and must be left to non-political agencies of social control. Relief from the burden of poverty, relief from want, relief from fear, insurance against frustration where men's ambition outruns their powers, are laudable humanitarian ideals. But much at least of the laudable humanitarian program, if not beyond practical attainment, is certainly beyond practical attainment through law.

III

THE AUTHORITARIAN PATH

I HAVE spoken of two paths: one a humanitarian path on which the law has entered and upon which it has made some progress, the other an authoritarian path, a path much more divergent from what our law has followed in the past. So far the authoritarian path is more suggested as the one still to be laid out than as yet actually taken; one which may go on parallel with the humanitarian path or which the humanitarian path may join to make the path of the future, or one of which the humanitarian path may prove but to be the beginning. Is our law moving now to secure a full life for everyone by a regime of shifting losses and imposition of liabilities according to greater ability to bear them? Or is it moving to do this through complete control by politically organized society of all individual activities and all productive exertion—through a regime of full services to everybody performed for us by politically organized society, as the path of the law in the service state? Another path was projected for a time, namely one of gradual disappearance of the regime of a legal order and complete substitution of an administrative order carried on before a hierarchy of bureau officials exercising discretion to achieve policies of service. It has been officially abandoned in Russia but perhaps more by giving up the name than by giving up the direction and *de facto* course of the path. The promoters of the service state are only partially resolving the paradox of nineteenth-century social individualism. That doctrine taught that a maximum of liberty was to be attained by a maximum of state control. Now we are taught that maximum of concern for the individual life calls for maximum satisfaction of the whole scale of human wants by a maximum of power of public officials over him. Yet the internal contradiction remains. For example, the service state is to relieve all feelings of inferiority and assure satisfaction of desires to move in the most esteemed social circles. So men are not to choose freely those who are to be in close association with them. They are not to be allowed to choose congenial companions for such intimate relations as in college fraternities or private rooming houses for college students, lest someone's social ambitions be frustrated, although the psychological tranquility from agreeable surroundings may be sacrificed as to others. One has to go back to the Laws of Manu for precedent for what is being urged upon fraternities and private dormitories in California today. According to Manu one who gave a banquet and did not invite his two nearest neighbors was subjected to a penalty.

As a lawyer I am not concerned with the service state nor with the omnicompetent state it threatens to become except as they indicate and indeed involve an authoritarian path for the law. Their general merits and demerits are for political scientist and economist. What I must think of is their effect upon the law and upon the legal profession. What this effect upon the law may be is illustrated whenever we read in the pronouncements of those who are urging transfer of the law to the authoritarian path about "socialization of law," "socialized courts," and "socialized procedure." In all these terms "socialized" is used to mean an extreme of unchecked power of officials and magistrates such as existed in the late totalitarian states and still obtains in Russia. Whether it is necessary to an adequate recognition and securing of social interests I doubt seriously. That it in practice follows hard in the wake of the service state and is characteristic of the authoritarian path thus far is undoubted. Coke boasted that there could be no infringement of the life or liberty or fortune or inheritance of an individual in England and no species of oppression or misgovernment at his expense but that it should be redressed in one or the other of the common-law courts. Today one of the leading exponents of the service state tells us that private law, the law which adjusts the relations of ordinary men and puts those who wield the authority of the state on the same plane with—not above—the ordinary man, is being swallowed up by a public law which puts the official on a higher plane.

A service state, a state which, instead of preserving peace and order and employing itself with maintaining the general security, takes the whole domain of human welfare for

its province and would solve all economic and social ills
through its activities, has made great progress toward establishing itself in this country after the first World War. It was
known earlier, from Roman law, in continental Europe and
was highly developed there in connection with the rise of
the great centralized nations of the world in and after the
sixteenth century. But, although some writers in England
were calling attention to its possibilities at the end of the
last century, it was so at outs with ingrained modes of legal
and political thought that few sought to fit the pieces of
evidence together to see what is indicated as to the direction
in which we have been moving. In the meantime it has
made exceedingly rapid progress and has covered already a
very wide field of individual activity and of official promo-
tion to broad welfare programs on every side.

I say service state rather than welfare state. The term
welfare state seems to me a boast. Governments have always
held that they were set up to promote and conserve public
welfare. This is implicit in the synonym "Commonwealth"
—the common weal or general welfare personified in the
state. So far men have agreed. But when it comes to the
question how the common weal or general welfare is to be
achieved, they have differed and do differ profoundly. Some
think the general welfare is best promoted by a government
which maintains order and administers justice by adjusting
relations and ordering conduct according to law, for the rest
leaving men to do things for themselves in their own way
so far as they do not commit aggressions upon others or subject others to unreasonable risk of injury, and act in good
faith in their relations with others. On the other hand there

have always been those who have believed in a benevolent government which helps men instead of leaving them free to help themselves; who have believed in a paternal order or paternal state (one might even say maternal state) doing things for subjects or citizens to the fullest extent.

Make it clear that I am not preaching against a service state in itself. The society of today demands services beyond those the state which only maintained order and repaired injuries could perform. In a complex industrial society it becomes more difficult to do by private initiative many things which the public wishes and wishes done quickly. Administrative agencies of promoting the general welfare have come to be a necessity and have come to stay. It would be futile to quarrel with the idea of a service state kept in balance with the idea of individual spontaneous initiative characteristic of the American. What one must question is not state performance of many public services which it can perform without upsetting our legal-political, economic and legal order, but the idea that all public services must and can only be performed by the government—that politically organized society and that alone is to be looked to for everything, and that there is no limit to the services to humanity which it can perform. What I challenge is carrying to the extreme the idea of regimented cooperation for the general welfare as the task of law; the exaltation of politically organized society to the position of an absolute ruler. This presupposes superman administrators and an all-wise majority or plurality, omnicompetent and equal to taking over the whole domain of the general welfare and to determining in detail what it calls for in every situation. The service state in the

English-speaking world began by performing a few major additional services beyond maintaining order and administering justice. As it has added more and more it has come to be jealous of public service performed by anyone else.

What is to be the effect of the service state upon our American constitutional legal polity? The service state as it develops as a super-state must be *par excellence* a bureau state. From the very nature of administration the bureau state calls for a highly organized official hierarchy. A hierarchy calls for a superman (very likely an *ex officio* superman) at its head. Thus it starts a path which may lead to a totalitarian state. The service state has Marxian Socialism and absolute government in its pedigree and has grown up along with the totalitarian state in other parts of the world. Liberty— free individual self-assertion, individual initiative, and self-help—is looked on with suspicion, if not aversion by the service state, and its advocates seek a "new concept of liberty" a freedom from want and freedom from fear, not freedom of self-assertion or self-determination. Self-help by the individual, competing with the service rendered by the state, seems an interference with the regime maintained by the government. Spontaneous individual initiative is frowned on as infringing on the domain of state action. The service state easily becomes an omnicompetent state, with bureaus of *ex officio* experts and propaganda activities carried on at public expense. If the step to it is gradual, the step from it to an absolute state is easy and may be made quickly.

Bills of rights are a characteristic feature of American constitutions. Beginning with the Virginia Bill of Rights of 1776, enacted immediately after the Declaration of Independence, they have been made a part of all our constitutions, state and federal. Our American bills of rights are prohibitions of government action infringing guaranteed rights, that is, guaranteed reasonable expectations involved in life in civilized society. They are laws, part of the constitution as the supreme law of the land, enforceable in legal proceedings in the courts at suit of those whose rights are infringed. They are generically distinct from the declarations of rights on the model of the French Declaration of Rights of Man which are to be found in constitutions outside the English-speaking world. These are mere preachments, declarations of good intentions or exhortations to governmental authority, legally binding on nobody and unenforceable by anyone whose interests are infringed. But the service state is beginning to affect our conception of a bill of rights in America. In a recent proposal for a declaration of rights for a world government we get the continental note in the very title, but also the note of the service state which is disinclined toward law. There is a declaration of a right of everyone everywhere to claim for himself "release from the bondage of poverty." It is not that he is to be free to free himself from this bondage, but that the state is to free him without his active help in the process. Also he is declared to have a right to claim reward and security according to his needs. But his claim to needs is likely to have few limits and is sure to conflict with claims of others to like needs. Such declarations are not merely preachments, not enforceable and not intended to be enforced as law; they are invitations to plundering by rapacious majorities or pluralities quite as much as to rapacious personal sovereigns.

In a recent book Professor Corwin has discussed the decadence of fear of oppression by government which has become very marked. Experience of government in seventeenth-century England and experience of government of the colonies from Westminster in the seventeenth and eighteenth centuries had made this fear a dominant consideration in our polity from the beginning till well into the present century. Growth of a feeling of the divine right of majorities, akin to that of divine right of kings, has led to an assumption that concern about oppression by government is something we have outgrown. Yet distrust of absolute majority or absolute plurality is as justified in reason and in experience as distrust of the absolute personal ruler. Indeed, the latter may be given pause by fear of an uprising which an intrenched majority need not fear.

It is characteristic of the service state to make lavish promises of satisfying desires which it calls rights. If a constitution promises to every individual "just terms of leisure," those who draft it do not ask themselves whether such a provision is a law, or part of the supreme law of the land, or a preachment of policy which no court can enforce and no legislative body can be made to regard. Such preachments enfeeble a whole constitutional structure. As they cannot be enforced, they lend themselves to a doctrine that constitutional provisions are not legally enforceable and may be disregarded at any time in the interest of political policy of the moment. They weaken the constitutional polity we have built up. Is there wealth enough in the world reachable by taxation imposed by a world government or even reachable by wholesale confiscation by a world state, to guarantee "just terms of leisure" during life to the whole population of the world or even to four hundred and fifty million Chinese?

Setting forth such things in a constitutional declaration of guaranteed rights makes a farce of constitutions. How can a government release the whole world through a political-legal process "from the bondage of poverty"? What organ of government can be made to bring about that enough is produced and is continuously produced to insure plenty for everyone everywhere? How can a court compel the legislature, the executive or an individual or organizations of individuals to bring this about, or how can the executive or the legislature compel either or anyone else to do it? Such pronouncements proceed upon a theory which used to be preached by social workers that law is a protest against wrong. Protests against wrong may be very effective in spurring lawmakers to find remedies and enact laws making the remedies effective. But protests themselves lack the qualities of enforceability and machinery of enforcement which are demanded for a law in any advanced society.

A power to act toward a general equality of satisfaction of wants and a policy of developing such an equality are something very different from a provision in a declaration of rights that a world government guarantees to bring such a policy to fruition. No one can seriously believe that in such a time as we can foresee the western world can provide social security to its furthest extent to the rest of the world, a great part of which is always close to the brink of starvation.

I have spoken at some length of proposals for declarations of rights for a world political organization because the propositions drafted by enthusiastic promoters of a world constitution are followed in recent proposals for constitution writing in the development of the service state in America. A state which endeavors to relieve its people of want and fear without being able to relieve its individual citizens of the many features of human make-up which lead to poverty and fear is attempting more than the miracles of science which has divided the indivisible have been equal to. How can we expect a state to bring about complete satisfaction of all the wants of everybody in a world in which we all want the earth and there is only one earth. Guarantees which are no more than promissory declarations of policy can do no more than deceive. The service state is a politically organized society and cannot, as could Baron Munchausen, pull itself up by its own long whiskers. This does not mean, however, that our nineteenth-century bills of rights cannot be supplemented to meet conditions of the urban industrial society of today.

Promissory bills of rights creating expectations of the politically and economically unachieveable and weakening faith in constitutions are a step toward the totalitarian state. The strong selling point of that state is its argument that a strong man, a superman leader, can do what a government hindered by constitutional checks and balances cannot do. When a constitution declares as rights claims to be secured by government which it cannot secure, it invites centralization of power in an absolute government which claims ability to secure them. The service state, taking over all functions of public service, operating through bureaus with wide powers, and little effective restrictions on their powers, through government positions for a large and increasing proportion of the population, and through systematic official propaganda and a system of subsidies to education, science and research, can easily be taking strides toward an absolute government, although under forms of democracy. Indeed the extreme advocates of the service state insist that constitutional democracy is a contradiction in terms. A democracy must be an unrestricted rule of the majority. The majority must be as absolute a ruler in all things as was the French king of the old regime or the Czar in the old regime in Russia. As the seventeenth century argued that a monarchy must in the nature of things be an absolute not a constitutional monarchy, on the same logical grounds it is argued that a democracy must be an absolute not a constitutional democracy.

General welfare service by the state, becoming service for strong aggressive groups or for politically powerful localities at the expense of the public at large, has been the ladder by which absolute rulers have climbed to power and the platform on which they have been able to stay in power. Louis XIV held down France by holding down Paris by distribution of bread at the expense of the provinces. The Spanish monarchy long held itself in power by using the wealth of the New World for service to its subjects at home. Napoleon III used state work shops. Totalitarian Italy used the theory of the service rendered by the corporative state. Totalitarian Russia promises proletariat rule at the expense of the rest of the community. Indeed in antiquity the Roman emperor held down Italy by extortion of wheat from Egypt.

Since the first World War we have preached a great deal and promised much as to the rights of minorities and of oppressed racial groups. But the lavish promises and administrative absolutism of the super-service state (or shall we say the service super-state?) with the absolute ultimate rule of majorities or even pluralities and of leaders in their name which they involve, are a menace to the guarantees that a constitution which is a legal document, not merely a frame of government promising welfare service which it cannot be made to perform, is able to give these groups. The attempt to make all men equal in all respects instead of in their political and legal rights and capacities is likely to make them more unequal than nature has made them already. Unless we give equality the practical meaning of our American bills of rights, we are likely to be thrown back to a proposition that all men are not born equal but are born equally.

There has been a tendency of men in all history to worship their rulers. In the society of today this takes the form of faith in absolute rule of the majority, or, indeed, of the plurality for the time being. We forget that majority or plurality are only a way out when we cannot get entire agreement. The founders of our polity, with long and bitter experience of absolute rule behind them, sought a government of checks and balances by which absolute rule by anyone was precluded. As Mr. Justice Miller put it, in the centennial year of the American Revolution, the theory of our governments, state and national, is opposed to the deposit of unlimited power anywhere. Today we are told that this doctrine is outmoded. What called for this pronouncement was legislation imposing a tax for subsidy to a private manufacturing enterprise. That was rejected as unconstitutional in 1875. But in the service state of today expensive service to some at the expense of others is regarded as a service to the public, as indeed it may be in some cases, and this tempts aggressive groups to obtain legislation providing service to them for which others must pay. A group of this sort easily in its own mind identifiies itself with the public. Obviously the conception of public service needs to be carefully defined and limited if we are to avoid being led into absolute rule by majority or plurality.

A government which regards itself, under pretext of extending a general welfare service to the public, entitled to rob Peter to pay Paul, and is free from constitutional restraints upon legislation putting one element or group of the people for the whole, has a bad effect on the morale of the people. If government is a device for benevolent robbery, a would-be Robin Hood of today is not likely to see why his benevolently conceived activities are reprehensible. Based on colonial experience of legislation imposing burdens on some for the benefit of others rather than of the public, our older state constitutions and substantially all state constitutions in the nineteenth century, forbade special or class legislation. The omission of this provision from recent constitutions is significant. No doubt the restriction in the nineteenth century constitutions was applied too rigidly and was at times made to stand in the way of proper welfare legislation. But entire omission points to a feeling that government is devised and intended to be unfair to minorities and that there should be no limit to the ability of organized groups to make their fellow man pay for special service to them.

A service state must be bureaucratic. Bureaus are characteristically zealous to get everything in reach under their control. Would it be a great public service to have a bureau of psychologists to examine us for our aptitudes, and assign us, whether we like it or not, to the calling for which they find us fitted? Before the advent of psychologists such a state was argued for by Greek philosophers. The later Eastern Roman empire stabilized society by putting and keeping men in callings somewhat in this way. An omnicompetent state postulates omnicompetent bureaus. Why in the perfect all-regulating state allow human energy to be wasted by permitting individuals to engage in futile efforts to employ themselves in callings in which they cannot succeed? Is that the next move after subsidizing them in callings in which they are failing and bound to fail?

Perhaps I have said enough to show that the authoritarian path indicated by the service state leads law away from law. At least it leads away from a legal order maintained by a judicial process adjusting relations and ordering conduct by applying authoritative models or patterns of decision. The end of social control is regarded as a broader end to be attained in administration without law.

Let us look next at what law pursuing the authoritarian path promises or threatens the profession of the lawyer. Let us turn to the effect of the service state upon the profession.

By a profession we have meant, until the rise to prominence of the professional athlete obscured our ideas, a group of men pursuing a common calling as a learned art and as a public service—none the less a public service because it may incidentally be a means of livelihood. From the standpoint of a profession there are three ideas: A common calling, a

learned art, and a spirit of public service. Gaining a livelihood is not a professional consideration. Indeed, the spirit
of a profession, the spirit of a public service constantly curbs
the urges of that incident. An organized profession does not
seek legislation relieving it of duties or liabilities incumbent
upon it. It does not seek to advance the money-making feature of professional activity. It seeks rather to make as effective as possible its primary character of a public service. An
engineer may patent his invention. A manufacturer may get
legal protection for his trade secret or patent his discovered
process. What a member of a profession invents or discovers
is not his property. It is at the service of the public.

Again a professional organization differs fundamentally
from a trade organization or an organization of men following a particular business or calling. It does not exist for the
benefit of those engaged in the calling but for the advancement of the public service which the profession is carrying
on. A bar association or an organized bar is not set up to
advance the financial condition of the lawyers but to further
the administration of justice by improving its agencies and
their operation in the light of experience and study. Nothing
could be more alien to the professional ideal than the
methods of organizations seeking by concerted action advancement of the individual members in disregard of the
interests of the public. A tradition of the duty of the lawyer
to the client, to the profession, to the courts, and to the
public, authoritatively declared in codes of professional
ethics, taught by precept and example and made effective by
the discipline of an organized profession exercised to uphold
the spirit of public service, not the remuneration of the

individual practitioners, makes for effective service to the public such as could not be had from individual practitioners not bred to the tradition and motivated, as in a trade, primarily, if not solely, by quest of pecuniary gain. This professional tradition cannot be replaced with benefit to the public by a political tradition of office holders owing primary allegiance to political parties and depending for advancement on the favor of political leaders. Moreover the professional organization and tradition are even more to the public interest in law and in medicine in their effect on the learned arts which the professions follow as callings.

Huge bureaus of graduates of law schools or of medical schools, brought up to seek public office and organized in the civil service as employees of the service state, can be no effective substitute for professions. When every form of public service becomes at least potentially a state function, the difference between a public service performed by a profession and a public function performed by a bureau becomes crucial.

If callings have making of a livelihood for their primary concern, in an economic order in which the great majority of the community are on the payroll of either the government or of some corporation, public, public-service, charitable or private, it follows that most individuals will be in a sense employees and so liable to be caught up in a regime of employees' organizations, of collective bargainings over wages, working conditions and pensions, and of strikes. Organization of physicians for advancement of medicine, organization of lawyers for advancement of justice, and organization of teachers for advancement of teaching must give way to organizations of employees of every grade and kind for advancement of wages and dictation of the conditions of employment. Already the two major labor organizations have announced a campaign to unionize the "white collar workers" in industry and business. This may well presently take in the younger members of the bar in the legal departments of great companies. Already the American Federation of Labor has organized municipal employees, and in Los Angeles the probation officers, whom we had been thinking of as members of a rising profession of social workers, are members of a Probation Officers' Union, a branch of a Municipal Employees' Union, affiliated with the national organization. Are the young lawyers in the offices of government legal departments, municipal, federal and state, to be taken in next and from time to time to strike for increased pay as collective bargain contracts expire or when one of their number is removed or discharged? Apparently we must say this is entirely possible. Every department and administrative agency of the federal government has many lawyers on its roster. Unions of federal employees may very likely seek to include them. The service state in its zeal to serve the employed by promoting organization and collective bargaining is threatening the general security by allowing them an extreme development.

Thus, as things are coming to be in the era of bigness, large-scale organization of all activities, and strenuous acquisitive competitive self-assertion, the professional idea must contend with the rise to power of organizers of an expanding class of employees. More and more, as individuals in the professions have come to be regularly retained or nowadays regularly employed by great corporations, or appointed to substantially permanent positions under the federal government or state and municipal governments and administrative agencies, a constantly larger number of practitioners in their capacity of employees are enlisted in organizations with the trade spirit of emphasis on wages rather than the professional idea of pursuit of a calling in the spirit of public service. This prevailing of the trade idea may, unless we are vigilant, make straight the path toward absorption of the professions in the service state. The course of that path is not hard to chart. We can see three possible stages: (1) Unionizing of all callings which may be taken to involve employment, at least so far as some in the calling are not capable of classification as employers; (2) getting control of professional education by government subsidies and thus subordinating the professions to bureaucratic management; (3) seeking to bring cheap professional assistance equally to everyone's back door by government taking over of the callings pursuing learned arts. Such a consummation may be pictured as a carrying of the idea of the service state to its furthest logical development. The service state began by performing a few major services. Now it has become jealous of public service being performed by any one else. The advocates of the omnicompetent state will say that in primitive or pioneer societies certain public services are rendered by anyone who seeks to try his hand on the basis of such qualification as he deems sufficient. Later, as society advances, such services are rendered by well qualified practitioners organized in professions, the qualifications, as these professions develop, being prescribed and ascertained by governmental authority. Ultimately, it will be said, as political organization of society reaches maturity, all public services of every description are to be exclusive governmental functions to be exercised by government bureaus.

Very likely not all of those who are teaching or preaching the doctrine of the super-service state will, at the moment, admit this. But I submit that before we go far with them on the path in which they are marching we should pause to see whither it leads.

Even more the professional ideal is menaced by the development of great government bureaus and a movement to take over the arts as practised by the professions and make them functions of the government to be exercised by its bureaus. An independent profession of lawyers is not looked on with favor by the thorough going bureaucrat. Already a proposition is urged that administrative agencies are to have their own body of practitioners to appear before them so that those against whom they proceed shall be held to representatives under the control of the tribunal and not, because of learning in the law and bringing up in the professional tradition of guarding the constitutional and legal rights of their clients, zealous to restrain administrative excesses by timely action and effective resort to all the remedies afforded by the law. Again, an article in a recent number of an important legal periodical attacked the mode pursued in qualifying those to be appointed trial examiners. The complaint is that the committee which advised was made up of one of the outstanding state judges of the land, a leader of the bar in one of our great cities, a former president of the American Bar Association, and a well known and able practitioner before administrative agencies who had much to do with formulating the Administrative Procedure Act. We are told that a body so composed is over-legalistic. It is sure to be too much inclined to expect trial examiners to be able to appreciate legal arguments, to keep within legal bounds, and to regards the means of obtaining them as important as well as the results.

Indeed the idea of a profession is incompatible with performance of the profession's function, exercise of its art, by or under the supervision of a government bureau. A profession presupposes individuals free to pursue a learned art so as to make for the highest development of human powers. The individual servant of a government exercising under its supervision a calling managed by a government bureau can be no substitute for the scientist, the philosopher, the teacher, each freely applying his chosen field of learning and exercising his inventive faculties and trained imagination in his own way, not as a subordinate in an administrative hierarchy, not as a hired seeker for what he is told to find by his superiors, but as a free seeker for the truth for its own sake, impelled by the spirit of public service inculcated in his profession.

If the path of liberty has ended or is to end in a blind alley, and if the humanitarian path is but a detour leading the law into the authoritarian path, the Marxian prophecy of the disappearance of law in the ideal society of the future is likely to be fulfilled. But I am unwilling to subscribe to the give-it-up philosophy that leads to this expectation. Instead I have faith that what was found for civilization while law was treading the path of liberty will not be lost. We shall not make a wholly new start in the humanitarian path. The humanitarian path will not be a mere by-pass to the authoritarian path. The path of the future will find a broader objective in the direction indicated by the humanitarian path. It will find a sure starting point where the path of liberty has seemed to end and will go forward toward the fullest development of human powers in what may prove to be a path of civilization. What has been worked out by experience and reason for the adjustment of relations and ordering of conduct toward the satisfaction of human claims and demands and expectations from the classical Roman jurists to the twentieth-century codes, from the King's Hall of Henry II to the Royal Courts of Justice of Victoria, from the courts of the American colonies to the constitutional system of American courts of today, is not to be wholly lost. Out of it, as the law pursues a broader and straighter path of civilization, should come a law of another great age of the law such as were the Roman classical era from Augustus to Alexander Severus and the maturity of the civil law on the Continent and of the common law in the English-speaking world in the nineteenth century.